GW00703499

and
Mental Health

by
Dr Pravin Thevathasan

*All booklets are published thanks to the
generous support of the members of the
Catholic Truth Society*

CATHOLIC TRUTH SOCIETY
PUBLISHERS TO THE HOLY SEE

Contents

All case histories described in this work have been modified out of respect for medical confidentiality.

All rights reserved. First published 2014 by The Incorporated Catholic Truth Society, 40-46 Harleyford Road London SE11 5AY Tel: 020 7640 0042 Fax: 020 7640 0046. Copyright © 2014 The Incorporated Catholic Truth Society.

ISBN 978 1 86082 918 5

Catholicism and Psychiatry

"If mental health enjoys such esteem in Catholic thought and practice, it is only right that the Church looks with satisfaction at the new path being opened by psychiatry…all that Sacred Scriptures say in praise of human wisdom are an implicit affirmation of the importance of mental health."

Pope Pius XII

This work aims to show that there should be no conflict between Catholicism and psychiatry. It is not intended as a treatment manual or a self-help guide and it will deal with a relatively small number of psychiatric disorders. It will examine depression in particular, as this is the commonest of the mental health disorders.

We will begin with a brief history of psychiatry, then examine the conflicts and agreements that have arisen between Catholicism and psychiatry, and end with an examination of some psychiatric disorders.

We will focus primarily on psychiatry even though psychiatry is but one area of mental health care.

A Brief History of Psychiatry

The ancient Greeks

The ancient Greeks tended to regard mental illness as a physical disorder that was due to the way the bodily humours of black bile, yellow bile, phlegm and blood are combined. According to this theory, every person is born with a predominance of one of these four humours, giving rise to the four temperaments. The melancholic is introverted with a tendency to depression, the choleric is extroverted and irascible, the phlegmatic is mild-mannered and the sanguine is optimistic. Melancholia was thought to be caused by an excess of black bile and was therefore regarded as a physical illness.

The great Hippocrates (460-377 BC) recognised and to some extent classified psychiatric disorders including delirium, hysteria and melancholia.

The Old Testament

Depression is powerfully described in, among other places, the Book of Job:

"If only my misery could be weighed,
And all my ills be put on scales!
But they outweigh the sands of seas;
What wonder then if my words are wild?" (*Jb* 6:2-3)

"And now the life in me trickles away,
Days of grief have gripped me.
At night time, sickness saps my bones,
I am gnawed by wounds that never sleep." (*Jb* 30:16-17)

The First Book of Samuel describes Saul as falling into depression, for which he was treated with soothing music (*1 S* 16:14-16). It was thought that Saul's madness was the result of sin and that both sin and insanity lead away from God, so the sick in mind needed a priest more than a doctor.

The ministry of Jesus

Jesus frequently described himself as a physician who has come to minister to the sick. Indeed some of the early Church Fathers such as St Clement of Alexandria speak of "Christ our physician." His healing ministry not only extended to the sinful but also to those with bodily illness.

Even in his time, many Jews held that illness was due to misdeeds of either the sufferer or his parents. While identifying with the Jews, it is apparent that Jesus does not attribute personal blame when bodily illness alone is considered. To the question posed by the disciples: "Rabbi, who sinned, this man or his parents that he should be born blind?" Jesus replied: "Neither he nor his parents sinned, he was born blind so that the works of God might be displayed in him" (*Jn* 9:3).

At the pool of Bethsaida, Jesus cures the man without a prior forgiveness of sins and says to him: "Sin no more in case something worse befalls you" (*Jn* 5:14). There is here a separation between personal sin and sickness. The consequence of unrepented sin is "something worse" than sickness.

The early Church

It is often assumed that the early Church regarded mental illness as being of demonic origin, but at no time was it suggested that possession was the only cause of mental illness. In fact the early Christian physicians accepted the teachings of Greek medicine while, unlike the Greeks, holding on to the principle of always treating even the incurable, for they too were sons and daughters of a loving God. Although some thought that mental illness ought to be treated by means of prayer and exorcism, this was not the general belief.

The early Christians established hospitals for medical and nursing assistance, and there was a form of Christian psychotherapy that was meant to be both therapeutic and consoling. Norman Auton, a hospital chaplain, suggested that the advances in the treatment of mental illness by the early Church were due to the great importance attached to individual and daily care.[1] The patient was loved, his personal dignity respected, and he was surrounded by an atmosphere of tender care. He was visited by the bishop, presbyters and deacons, and blessed at the Eucharist. The treatment of the early Church was based on a philosophy of hope and was therefore helpful and encouraging. It aimed to conquer fear and establish peace of soul; many converts received these blessings after rejecting paganism and realising that the world is not dominated by evil forces but has come from the hands of a loving God.

In the second century AD, the Cappadocian physician Aretaeus gave a fascinating description of the depressed patient:

> "Those affected with melancholy are not every one of them affected according to one particular form…. [T]he patients are dull or stern, dejected or unreasonably torpid…. [U]nreasonable fear also seizes them, if the disease tends to increase…they complain of life and desire to die."[2]

The history of psychiatry might have been quite different had this advancement in care for the mentally ill at the beginning of Christianity continued.

The Middle Ages

When the barbarian hordes invaded the Roman Empire, there was a general decline of civilisation and a corresponding decline in the practice of medicine. However, towards the end of the twelfth century, a new conception of human nature appeared which stressed the unity of mind and body:

"So knit was the unity of man that whatever affected one part of him affected all the rest…. St Thomas Aquinas frequently referred to psychosomatic interactions: the excesses of passion which sicken the body and disorder the mind, the vehement perceptions of the mind which stir the emotions and alter the body's functions, the diseases of the body which influence mind, spirit, imagination and feelings. These concepts would naturally indicate that mental ills belong in the domain of the physician."[3]

These were times of great contradiction. On the one hand mentally ill patients were persecuted, and on the other hand they were treated with love and care, as in Gheel, Belgium, where, under the supervision of the Church, they were cared for in the townspeople's homes and participated fully in family life. Gheel was under the patronage of St Dymphna, patron saint of the mentally ill.

Hospitals for the mentally ill were established by Pope Innocent III and by the Order of St John of Jerusalem among others. In England, the priory of St Mary of Bethlehem was founded in 1247 by Simon Fitzmary. By 1403, it had become a well-known hospital for the mentally ill, the precursor of the famous Bethlehem Hospital. It is interesting to note that a number of people were admitted with the specific intention of being discharged when better.

Gilbetus Anglicus (1180-1250) in his *Compendium Medicinae* described auditory and visual hallucinations as well as phobias. He suggested that treatment ought to include the building up of self-confidence and the development of a therapeutic relationship with the patient.

Pope John XXI (1200-1277) said that psychology belonged to the natural sciences, as did St Thomas Aquinas (1225-1274).

Bernard de Gordon (1260-1318) classified melancholia into different stages: hidden melancholia, outward melancholia and complete melancholia leading to social withdrawal.

Witch trials

Unfortunately, alongside these positive developments, the fourteenth and fifteenth centuries saw outbursts of witch hunts, when mental illness and behaviours deemed eccentric were sometimes confused with witchcraft. The differences were understood in principle but not always in practice. What is certain is that there were charlatans who played on the superstitions of the common folk for personal profit. These witch trials were to continue after the Reformation in Catholic and Protestant regions.

The humane response

In the midst of these tragic events, there were voices of reason. Johann Weyer (1515-1588) was a brilliant physician whom many regard as the true founder of modern psychiatry. In his work *De Praestigis Daemonum* he concluded that so-called witches were generally mentally ill people in need of medical treatment. A devout Catholic, he condemned the witch trials: "It is highly unpleasant to see how people, in the name of killing errors, are busy killing human beings."

The twentieth century Catholic psychiatrist Gregory Zilboorg credited Weyer with the discovery of the power of imagination and the role of fantasy in the formation of symptoms of mental illness.

Weyer's teacher Cornelius Agrippa of Nettesheim (1486-1535) also condemned the witchcraft trials as did the famous Paracelsus (1493-1541).

The Spaniard Juan Luis Vives (1492-1540), friend of St Thomas More, was a devout Catholic and a highly educated man. He defended the status of women at a time when many were subjected to the vilification of the witch hunters. He urged humane treatment for the inmates of mental asylums and condemned the unnecessary use of restraint. His observations have earned for him the title of father of modern empirical psychology.

Reginald Scott, an Englishman, came to the same conclusion as Vives and published *The Discovery of Witchcraft* in 1584 in which he wondered how so many people could be deceived into believing that the mentally ill were witches. Unfortunately, King James I ordered the book to be burned and so the deception continued.

St Vincent de Paul

St Vincent de Paul (1580-1660) also recognised that many so-called witches were mentally ill. The hospital of St Lazare in Paris was founded by the Vincentians in 1632.

St Vincent wrote that "mental disease is no different from bodily disease. Christianity demands of the humane and the powerful to protect and the skilful to relieve the one as well as the other."[4]

A Vincentian priest has written a useful summary of St Vincent's method of treating the mentally ill:

1. He tried to ensure optimum physical health.

2. He used the absolute minimum of restraint.

3. He asked such patients to make use of confession in order to relieve their mind of anxiety.

4. He tried to re-educate them by individual counselling and advice.

5. He gave them, where possible, congenial and rewarding work to do.

6. He aimed at completing their contact with reality by re-orientating their emotions from self towards God and neighbour.[5]

To sum up, from the beginning the Christian response to mental suffering has been far more compassionate and caring than is widely assumed. The mediaeval treatment of the mentally ill was far from perfect, but there were humane responses throughout the period.

When Psychiatry and Catholicism Conflict

"Psychiatrists have not increased the credibility of their speciality in the first three quarters of the twentieth century by posing as the universal experts on the experience of life and how it should be led. Expert knowledge of the abnormal does not preclude ignorance of the normal and the psychiatrist can never generalise from the sample of people selectively referred to him to the whole of mankind."[6]

Professor Andrew Sims,
past President of the Royal College of Psychiatrists

The author believes that this has been the single most important statement to affect his own understanding of the relationship between psychiatry and Catholicism. We have seen how harmful it was for some Christians to confuse mental illness with witchcraft. We shall now examine what happens when psychiatrists and others in the field of mental health pose as the "universal experts on the experience of life and how it should be led." Two such individuals were Sigmund Freud and Carl Jung; their work will be examined in some detail as they have been highly influential in the field of psychiatry. The section will end with an assessment of other areas of human life where some psychiatrists posed as universal experts and failed.

When the theories of Freud and Jung are examined, they often appear to be based on belief systems rather than on scientific evidence. The eminent psychiatrist Emil Kraepalin said in 1921 that Freud's theories were "arbitrary assumptions and conjectures assumed as facts". However, the mysteries surrounding their therapies continued to fascinate people at a time when organised religion was in decline. They also appeared to offer a world-view that addressed modern alienation. By the 1980s, their theories had fallen largely out of favour to be replaced by a more robustly scientific version of psychiatry that was evidence-based. However, they continue to appeal to the spiritually minded and to academics interested in the humanities.

Christianity According to Sigmund Freud

Sigmund Freud was born in Moravia in 1856. His early childhood was, to say the least, somewhat unorthodox. His mother was his father's third wife and was younger than the elder son from the first marriage. His stepbrother Philip was apparently attracted to Freud's mother. Freud was later to recall a famous event when he felt disgusted towards his father, and he was also to admit to feelings of guilt after wishing that a younger brother would die - an event which actually occurred. So, his later bizarre notions of childhood sexuality may be related to his own childhood experiences. Ernest Jones, his biographer and friend, maintained that these odd family circumstances together with Freud's misconstruing of them facilitated Freud's greatest discovery, the Oedipus complex. There are even suggestions that Freud had been sexually abused, a point mentioned in a book by the psychologist Professor Paul Vitz, which will be discussed later.

There is little doubt that Freud was an exceptional student. However, there was no place for religion in his early life. His interest in philosophy culminated in a study of Darwin's theory of evolution, which led him, in turn, to study medicine. He continued with his philosophical studies, taking a particular interest in the works of Ludwig Feuerbach who in his *Essence of Christianity* wrote that men have created God and heaven as a means of fulfilling their own wishes. God is, according to Feuerbach, merely a projection of all that is excellent in human nature.

Psychoanalysis

Freud is now best known for his psychoanalytical method. It has been recognised that there are similarities between psychoanalysis and the occult doctrines of the Kabbalah. They both share an emphasis on male and female elements, a fixation with numbers, and the exploration of a variety of symbols. Some fundamental themes can be found in the *Zohar* or *Book of Splendour* (which contains the teachings of the Kabbalah), such as bisexuality, malevolent childhood impulses and dream interpretations.

Freud was also deeply interested in witchcraft and other occult phenomena. On Saturday evenings, he would frequently play tarock - a card game associated with the Kabbalah. However, he appeared to have a conscious hatred of religion - both Orthodox Judaism and Christianity. In 1937, when he was urged to flee Nazism, he responded that his real enemy was the Roman Catholic Church. Interestingly enough, his childhood hero was Hannibal, the Carthaginian besieger of Rome.

Freud was also to make sure that his wife rejected Jewish orthodoxy soon after they were married. Religion was for him nothing but psychology projected into the external world. Biologically speaking, religion is to be traced back to the small child's long drawn-out helplessness. The longing for the Father that constitutes the root of every form of religion inevitably calls up the entanglement of the Oedipus complex, including feelings of fear and guilt.

Freud and religion

By 1907, Freud was writing papers that were deeply hostile to religion, claiming that there were similarities between neurotic behaviour and religious rituals. This observation was based on his study of a handful of disturbed patients.

In 1913, he wrote *Totem and Taboo*. According to this work, primitive societies had established certain taboos including prohibitions designed to prevent sexual relations between members of the same clan. As with neurosis, this gives rise to ceremonial acts of expiation, penance and purification. Freud based his whole theory of Totemism on the controversial beliefs of W. Robertson Smith. According to this theory, brothers got together to kill their dictatorial father who kept them away from women. They were then filled with guilt and revoked their deed by forbidding the killing of the Totem - typically an animal, the substitute for their father. This Totem religion preserves the ambivalence implicit in the Oedipus complex. The Christian doctrine of the Atonement represents an acknowledgement of the guilty primeval deed. Christ's sacrifice leads to reconciliation with God the Father. The crime to be atoned for is patricide and the revival of the ancient totemic meal is to be found, according to Freud, in the Eucharist.

Of course, it goes without saying that not one shred of evidence is offered for these conjectures. His book *Moses and Monotheism* is a truly extraordinary work of fantasy. According to Freud, Moses was really an Egyptian - probably from an aristocratic family. He believed in worshipping the one God, the sun god Aten. When the Egyptians denounced him, he turned to the Jews whom he chose as his people. They left Egypt but the people were not able to tolerate this highly spiritual religion and they therefore murdered Moses. Several generations later, the Jews came under a new religion devoted to the worship of Yahweh, a bloodthirsty demonic volcano god. A new Moses, this time a Jewish one, became a substitute for the Egyptian one and the new god Yahweh is given credit for having liberated his people from Egypt. Just to show that Yahweh had been with his people all along, the legends of Abraham, Isaac and Jacob are introduced. Remorse for having killed the Egyptian Moses creates a longing for a Messiah.

Again, where is the evidence for any of this? When Freud was told that there was no replacement Moses, he responded: "And yet, it might be true for it fits so well into the frame of my thesis!"

In 1927 came his most famous attack on religion - *The Future of an Illusion*. The question asked is: can we one day do without the consoling illusions of religious beliefs? Religious beliefs are based, according to Freud, on desires that cannot be challenged and they lie in the infantile past of the individual when he sought protection from the mother and father. Later on, our fear of death will bring back the old anxieties and the longing to be protected by the father. This irrational origin of religion gives it the odour of sanctity but it has proved unhelpful to most people: "The question cannot but arise whether we are not overrating its necessity for mankind."

Freud thought that if you introduce religion to children before the age of reason, it would lead to a prohibition of thought and neurotic control of impulses through repression: "Religion is patently infantile, so foreign to reality. It is painful to think that the great majority of men will never be able to rise above this view of life." So for Freud, religion needs to be replaced by science.

The Christian Freud?

What does this preoccupation with themes such as wanting the death of the father and childhood sexuality tell us about the human condition? Very little. What does it tell us about Freud? Why is he so hostile towards Christianity? In order to answer these questions, Freud himself needs to undergo analysis.

Some years ago, Paul Vitz wrote a fascinating book entitled *Sigmund Freud's Christian Unconscious*[7] in which he argues that Freud had a largely unconscious attraction towards Catholicism. His mother related how as a child, after he was taken by his nanny to church, "you came home and you used to preach to us about God". Freud described himself later as being like a monk in his cell offering secular pastoral counselling, he encouraged his daughter to pick flowers for Our Lady and he wrote of his longing to be in Rome for Easter. He once blurted out: "Only Catholicism protects us against Nazism." In all sincerity, he said of psychoanalysis: "I don't think our cures can compare to those at Lourdes."

These comments are hardly typical of an atheist. The Catholic psychiatrist Gregory Zilboorg concluded: "Religion was for Freud a field of which he knew very little and which, moreover, seems to have been the very centre of his inner conflicts, conflicts that were never resolved."

Vitz also deals with Freud's self-identification with the person of the Antichrist and with Velikovsky's thesis (made in 1941) that Freud had made a Faustian pact. Freud himself wrote that if he had his life to live again, "I would devote myself to psychical research rather than psychoanalysis."

Freud's own followers were largely unaware of his own inner conflicts and they further refined his anti-religious sentiments. For example, with regard to what they perceive as the creation myth: the serpent in the Garden of Eden tempting Eve is to be regarded merely as a symbol of the maturing sex drive. For the psychoanalyst Ludwig Levy, the Genesis story is deliberately anti-sexual so that religion can be freed from the fertility rites and pagan tradition where the serpent was revered as divine. For the psychoanalyst Theodore Reik, the paradise story consists of the murder of Yahweh, a tree god, the totem substitute for the murdered father. Reik also claimed that Cain did not really kill Abel - in fact, he committed incest with his mother and murdered his father.

For the traditional psychoanalyst, the great fish in the story of Jonah is a symbol of his mother, and the command to rest on the Sabbath equates with avoiding any action affecting Mother Earth and is thus a defence against incestuous tendencies. There is thus a constant reduction of sacred tradition to sexual and aggressive impulses.

Morality

How does psychoanalysis relate to morality? For psychoanalysts, there are no absolute moral principles since one's moral actions are determined by unconscious motives. If I were to give to the poor, my conscious intention is to do good. But unconsciously I may have evil intentions such as desiring to be famous. A believer in Freudian morality would thereby justify not giving to the poor, as the unconscious motives may be sinful.

Psychoanalysts believe in psychic determinism. If the ex-president of the United States chooses to commit adultery, this is not really his fault. It has been brought about by certain childhood experiences and he is therefore sick, not vicious. Freud held a Hobbesian view of man as a being whose dangerous instincts must be restrained through therapy.

Psychoanalysis had a disastrous effect on the twentieth century. Men undergoing therapy were told that they were unconsciously homosexual, husbands were advised to divorce and wives were told to find lovers. But how reliable are these so-called unconscious activities? Freud, for example, read an account that Leonardo Da Vinci was attacked by a bird, in which the word was mistranslated as "vulture". From this, and by dwelling on Egyptian mythology, Freud concluded that Leonardo was homosexual. The bird was, in fact, a kite.

In the early 1960s, academics under Freud's influence sought to change sexual morality in order to prevent, as they thought, a breakdown in civilisation. They encouraged therapeutic adultery and sex education, with no sexual deviation excluded. Freud's theory of the death instinct was popularised in films and plays because it was thought that the enactment of cruelty and aggression would lead to a catharsis and to a less violent society.

There are remarkable similarities between Karl Marx and Freud. They both held religion to be an illusion and neither believed in the existence of an immortal soul. They both shared assumptions about man and the world that are grounded in the philosophy of the Enlightenment. They were also completely under the influence of the theories of Charles Darwin. Freud wrote: "Just as the body in its developmental stages shows traces of earlier phases in the evolution of mankind, so may the unconscious be regarded as in some respects a repository of past experiences in the early mental development of mankind."

Freudian fallacy

In an interesting work entitled *The Freudian Fallacy*[8] E.M. Thornton wrote: "Freud's concept of the unconscious must be attributed to his cocaine usage. Death wishes, infantile incestuous desires and perversion are not the preoccupations of the normal mind. Constantly recurring throughout the drug literature are the same words and phrases used by Freud and his followers to describe his concept of the unconscious mind. In both psychoanalysis and this literature the same metaphors of looking down into an abyss occur."

After all, in *The Future of an Illusion*, Freud wrote: "Among the instinctive wishes of mankind are those of incest, cannibalism and lust for killing." And in his famous *Interpretation of Dreams* he wrote: "I was making frequent use of cocaine to reduce some troublesome nasal swellings."

If he had nasal swellings, he was almost certainly using cocaine frequently. Whatever one's view of the cocaine hypothesis, it would appear that in accepting his theories without due discernment, we have to a certain extent plunged Christianity and culture into chaos. If Rogerian man (that is, man according to psychologist Carl Rogers), innocent of original sin and naturally good, is capable of salvation without grace, Freudian man, in contrast, is utterly depraved, riddled with guilt feelings from childhood and incapable of making a good moral act. We move from Pelagianism to Jansenism.

The Church has surely been wise to treat certain aspects of psychotherapy with great caution.

Carl Jung's Journey from God

Jung's theories have penetrated more deeply inside certain Catholic circles than those of any other therapist. There is an apparent mystical aura surrounding his name when compared to the overt atheism of Freud or the humanism of Carl Rogers. Spiritual retreats inspired by him are still popular and his doctrines are even to be found in popular culture, such as the Star Wars films, which may in part, be regarded as Jungian adventure in outer space.

Jung was born in 1875. His father was a Lutheran pastor and his mother came from a spiritualist background. His childhood was lonely and unhappy and he developed a vivid fantasy life in compensation. He was extremely observant and was concerned with his parents' marital problems and with his father's growing loss of faith. His parents' marital problems seem to have stemmed from their vastly different personalities. His father was an introvert who suffered from bouts of depression and his mother was lively and jovial with an unhealthy interest in the occult. He attempted to communicate his own experiences of God to his father in an attempt to restore his father's faith. Unfortunately he was not successful as relations between father and son were poor and because Jung himself was to lose his faith in orthodox Christianity at a very early age. Nevertheless, he was to have a lifelong interest in the effect that religion has on people. The precocious Jung would ask himself questions such as: Why did God arrange things so that Adam and Eve would disobey him? Why did he command a father to kill his son? Indeed, the Abraham-Isaac motif is significant in view of his own ambivalent relationship with his father.

As a child he developed scruples, believing that a lot of his thoughts were blasphemous. He eventually concluded that God wanted him to have these thoughts just as he wanted Adam and Eve to fall. Again, this is deeply significant as Jung was later to believe that wholeness meant integrating the good and evil parts of one's personality.

Apart from his father, Jung had eight uncles who were clergymen and it was therefore expected that he would also be called to the ministry. However, by then he had developed an interest in philosophy and he decided to study medicine in order to become a psychiatrist.

At medical school, he developed an interest in Spiritualism. His doctoral thesis was a study of a young medium, a cousin of his, who in her trance claimed that she was possessed by the personality of a much older man.

In 1907, Jung published his work *The Psychology of Dementia Praecox*. Sigmund Freud became interested and invited him to Vienna. The two met and a strong emotional relationship developed between them. Jung saw in Freud the much needed father-figure and Freud was at first to regard Jung as his natural successor in the psychoanalytical movement. He was Freud's close collaborator for a period of five years between 1907 and 1912. However, it all ended acrimoniously when Jung disagreed with Freud's belief in the sexual basis of neurosis. The authoritarian Freud was most certainly unimpressed by this dissent.

Jung and the occult

Following this break with Freud, Jung came close to a mental breakdown. He deliberately allowed his irrational side to function freely and he kept detailed notes of his strange experiences, dreams and visions. Certainly many strange events were reported around this time. His house felt haunted, his daughters claimed to have seen ghosts and he himself saw a crowd of spirits bursting into the house. As they disappeared, he went into a three-day state of automatic writing leading to the production of his work entitled *The Seven Sermons*.

Jung was visited by a "spirit guide" whom he named Philemon, a "pagan who brought with him an Egypto-Hellenistic atmosphere with a Gnostic coloration". Although he may have suggested that the spirit guide was a figment of his imagination, in truth, as far as he was concerned it was a real being, "an old man with the horn of a bull. I was walking up and down the garden with him and to me he was what the Indians call a Guru." He also became acquainted with another spirit guide named Ka. "Ka's expression had something demonic about it - one might almost say Mephistopholean." This is a highly pertinent observation as Jung, like Freud, was fascinated by the Faust-Mephistopheles legend about the doctor who sold his soul to the devil in order to obtain secret knowledge. Jung had by now obtained a whole series of messages from his spirit guides, which were to determine the nature of his beliefs. The Jungian expert Dr Anthony Storr concluded: "Jung thought of these spirit guides as existing in an imperishable world and manifesting themselves from time to time through the psyche of an individual."[9]

Jung on religion

He developed an interest in religion, or at least his particular version of religion. For religion to be authentic, he felt, it must not be divorced from the unconscious. This interest led him to reading works by alchemists. For him, their obscure texts were expressions of unconscious fantasies. He wrote: "The experience of the alchemists was in a sense my experience and their world was my world. The possibility in a comparison with alchemy and the uninterrupted intellectual chain back to Gnosticism gave substance to my psychology." This is the key to Jungian psychology, to his belief that the unconscious fantasies are universal and that they can appear at any age in a similar form. They are, for him, the basis of religious expression. The dogmas of the Trinity, the Mass and the personality of Christ may all be seen and understood as expressing essential aspects of the human psyche. If these symbols are allowed to remain unconscious we are not really whole. The process of becoming whole is known as 'individuation', the central idea of his psychology. In cases of patients who had lost their faith, individuation led them to create their own myths as expressed through dreams and fantasy, and enabled them to gain wholeness.

Jung's concept of psychological truth is thus unscientific. For him, because a belief is invested with great emotional meaning, it must be true. Dogma is nothing more than something irrational expressed through the imagination. He was not interested in objective truth, only subjective fantasies.

According to Jung, the psyche has three levels: the conscious, the personal unconscious and the collective unconscious. The outermost crust of one's personality is the persona, that part of our personality which is exposed to the outer world. The unconscious mind is, as it were, the mirror image of the conscious mind. In other words, the very masculine person is unconsciously strongly feminine, the timid man unconsciously brave and so on.

The personal unconscious is a relatively insignificant fraction of the total unconscious material. That which lies below the personal unconscious is known as the collective unconscious, which contains the collective beliefs and

myths of the race to which the person belongs. The deepest
levels of the collective unconscious are known as the
universal unconscious, common to all human beings, even
to man's primitive and animal ancestry.

For Jung, the collective unconscious is not simply
a theory. It really exists. His system of psychotherapy
is based on bringing the patient into contact with the
healing collective unconscious through, for example, the
interpretation of dreams.

'Archetype' is another term which occurs frequently
in Jungian theory. Archetypes are alleged to be inborn
forms of intuition which lead us to experience life in a
manner conditioned by the past history of mankind. These
archetypal images include gods and goddesses, dwarves
and giants, or they may appear as fantastic or real animals
and plants.

On Christianity

What was his attitude towards Christianity? In answering
this, one must always remember that wholeness for him
is only possible when we integrate the negative shadow
and dark side with the more acceptable, conscious ego.
In other words the pursuit of goodness cannot lead to
wholeness. In his work *Psychology and Alchemy*, Jung
wrote: "Christian civilization has proved hollow to a
terrifying degree. The inner man has remained untouched.
His soul is out of key with his external beliefs." Wholeness

and not holiness is what matters. Christian civilisation has failed owing to a lack of psychological culture. It is psychology that "opens people's eyes to the real meaning of dogmas. Too few have experienced the divine image as the innermost possession of their soul." His ambivalence towards Christianity is seen when on the one hand he recommends his patients to return to the Church to which they belonged and on the other hand he writes: "there is no Deity, no submission or reconciliation to a Deity. The place of the Deity seems to be taken by the whole man." The 'whole man' realises his brotherhood with all living things, even with inorganic matter and the cosmos itself. The whole man must achieve three things. Firstly, he must meet with his shadow and learn to live with the more terrifying aspect of himself. Secondly, he must meet with the archetypes of the collective unconscious, especially through dream work. Thirdly, if he is fortunate enough, he will in the end find that pearl of great price, the archetype of wholeness, the self.

Jung claimed to have identified three stages of religious evolution. The first stage was the archaic age of the shamans. This was followed by the ancient civilisation of prophets and priests. Then came the Christian heritage of mystics. At every stage of religious history, all human beings share in the inner divinity, the 'numinous'. When Jung talks about God, he is really talking about the god within, the self. He was once asked if he believed in God.

He answered: "I don't believe. I know." Thus Jung made an act of faith in the existence of the collective unconscious and in archetypes and he interpreted Christianity in the light of his beliefs. As an example, let us examine the doctrine of the Trinity. For Jung, this doctrine is replete with psychological meaning. The Father symbolises the psyche in its original undifferentiated wholeness. The Son represents the human psyche, and the Holy Spirit the state of self-critical submission to a higher reality. For this myth to be authentic it must be found in other cultures, and Jung found similar Trinitarian ideas in the Babylonian Egyptian and Greek mystical traditions.

However, he believed in a Quaternity, the fourth person being the principle of evil. Without the opposition of Satan, who, for Jung, is one of God's sons, the Trinity would have remained a unity. In Jungian terms, without the opposition of the shadow or the fourth person, there would be no psychic development and no actualisation of the self. Jung came to believe that Mary became the fourth person following her Assumption. She is the necessary feminine element, the opposition of the shadow.

Wholeness

His idea of wholeness means that God approves of evil. He wrote: "Since I knew from experience that God was not offended by blasphemy, that on the contrary, he could encourage it, because he wished to evoke not only man's bright and positive side but also his darkness and ungodliness, God in his omniscience arranged everything so that Adam and Eve would sin. God intended them to sin." Thus Jung blames God for the fall of Adam and Eve. He causes them to sin because he himself is both good and evil. In his essay on Job, Jung contended that Yahweh desired the love of mankind but behaved like a thoughtless and irritable tyrant, indifferent to human misery. Like Adam who is mythically married to Lilith, daughter of Satan, and Eve, so is Yahweh married to Israel and to Sophia, who compensates for Yahweh's behaviour by showing human beings the mercy of God. Her appearances in the visions of Ezekiel and Daniel lead to a fundamental change. God transforms himself by becoming man. Yahweh has wronged the creatures who have outdone him and only by becoming man can he atone for his injustice.

Jung appears to have lost his faith during his childhood. He wrote: "Lord Jesus Christ was to me unquestionably a man and therefore a fallible figure." Maintaining a tradition put forward by Gnostics, he believed that Christ is the symbolic representation of the most central archetype, the self. However, the sublime goodness of Christ means that, from a psychological perspective, he lacks wholeness. Missing is the dark side of the psyche, the element of evil. Christ receives wholeness in the person of the Antichrist.

Jung on Christ

The Church teaches that Christ died in order to save us. For Jung, this is a misleading rationalisation for an otherwise inexplicable act of cruelty. The angry Yahweh of the Old Testament is full of guilt and is in need of atonement. Jesus dies on Calvary to expiate the sins of God the Father.

We will conclude by way of quotes from three eminent psychiatrists. The Catholic psychiatrist Dr Rudolph Allers wrote: "For Jung, God is not a transcendent reality of whom man may achieve some knowledge by natural reason but, rather, an archetype, a basic tendency in human nature. The idea of God and of a future life is not seen as expressing reality but as a corresponding subjective need."

Dr Gregory Zilboorg observed: "That which Jung calls religion is not a religion at all. Even from an empirical point of view, it appears to be only a very incidental manifestation."

Dr Anthony Storr wrote: "A good deal of Jungian psychology can be seen as Jung's attempt to find a substitute for the orthodox faith in which he was reared, but against which he started to rebel at a very early age."

Our rejection of the theories of Freud and Jung have been based on our rejection of their belief systems and not on any scientific evidence that they have come up with.

The Nature of Apparitions

The conflicts between Catholicism and psychiatry are not limited to the theories of Jung and Freud. Let us examine how some mental-health experts have attempted to understand extraordinary phenomena as they have occurred in Catholic history. Helen Deutsch, a famous colleague of Sigmund Freud, wrote this about St Bernadette of Lourdes: "Bernadette turns away from reality and abandons herself to fantasy which she experiences with hallucinatory intensity…. 'The Lady' is a product of fantasy."[10]

This is so far off the mark that no response is really required. A tongue-in-cheek response to this kind of analysis was made by Fr Felix Duffey:

"Joe Deakes, as a little boy, is kicked in the pants by his grandmother for something that his older brother Eustace did. After forty years of repressing his emotions, he begins to denounce the Knights of Columbus and other fraternal orders. One day a beggar says to him 'Brother, can you spare me a dime?' and he violently attacks the chap."[11]

Other humorous commentators on the same theme have included Ronald Knox, Fulton Sheen and, of course, G.K. Chesterton. More seriously, a complete repudiation of the supernatural is clearly not a good basis for dialogue between psychiatry and Catholicism.

The psychiatrist is certainly not in a position to discuss the authenticity of apparitions, locutions and other extraordinary phenomena. His contribution in the process of discernment is to differentiate between those who are mentally ill and those who are not. In doing so, he may consider some of the following points:

1. The mentally ill person may have other symptoms of mental illness. He may draw attention to himself. This contrasts with the behaviour of St Bernadette who went out of her way to avoid publicity.

2. Mental illness involving hallucination is characterised by disordered thinking and loss of goal-directed activity.

3. Extraordinary manifestations are not treated with sensible caution by the mentally ill. In contrast, authentic seers are prepared to await further judgement.

4. The mentally ill person does not have much reticence in talking about his experiences. He is often surprised by the incredulity of others.

It is worth noting that the number of apparitions accepted by the Church is small in comparison to the claims made, even though the majority of claimants are not mentally ill. The teaching of St John of the Cross is salutary and may be summed up as follows: "One should take no notice of visions and revelations, but live one's spiritual life in faith, hope and charity. If the alleged visions are divine, Almighty God will see to it if he wishes that this become abundantly clear."[12]

On Sanctity

Psychiatrists have no special expertise in understanding the interior life and if they attempt to arrive at general conclusions from a study of their patients, they are likely to get it wrong. For example, the eminent psychiatrist Ernst Kretschmer (1888-1964) attempted to interpret self-denial in the following manner: "Those who practice self-denial develop pleasure from the denial of their appetites...a perversion of instinctive urges."[13]

The pastoral wisdom of centuries is thus dismissed in a sentence because the psychiatrist attempted to draw general conclusions from select patients and possibly from his own preconceived ideas.

Similar consequences occur when psychiatrists try to understand mystical states from a purely psychological perspective. The psychiatrist Professor Frank Fish in his well-known textbook of psychopathology described one of St Teresa of Avila's mystical experiences as: "Probably the result of a lack of sleep, of hunger and religious enthusiasm."[14]

In fact, St Teresa was extremely prudent in all matters relating to "enthusiasm" and extraordinary phenomena. Far from being an enthusiast, she was remarkable for her practical common sense and peace of soul amidst tribulations. Much the same might be said of St Catherine of Siena (1347-1380) and St Joan of Arc (1412-1431), both of whom have been described as unbalanced in some psychiatric textbooks.

The truth lies in the observation that: "With regard to the phenomena of mysticism in its proper sense, psychopathology has nothing to offer, and for the very good reason that infused contemplation is brought about by grace, which does not destroy, but perfects and elevates the natural capacities."[15]

Catholicism and psychiatry: a need for dialogue

We will try to show in subsequent sections that the mentally ill person not infrequently needs both medical and spiritual help in order to have his health restored. Psychiatry alone cannot heal a wounded heart or cleanse a sinful one:

"When speaking of the priest's contribution to mental health, one's thoughts turn first to his function as confessor. Now confession in the Catholic sense has a therapeutic value all its own, but it cannot be compared with any other therapeutic device since confession is a sacrament and therefore belongs to the supernatural order. Those who look upon sacramental confession as just another psychotherapeutic device miss its meaning completely…[A]lthough confession belongs to the supernatural order, it has psychotherapeutic after-effects, for it not only rids the penitent of his sins but greatly contributes in most cases to his feelings of security by ridding him of his feelings of guilt… [M]any a person tortured by guilt feelings due to perfectly conscious sins confides to the Priest: 'If this had gone on much longer, I believe it would have driven me crazy.' Hence confession may help to prevent the occurrence of mental disease."[16]

We may confidently say that, for some cases, religion and psychiatry are not in conflict: the treatment of mental illness is helpful to, but no substitute for, the cure of the soul.

When Psychiatry and Catholicism Agree

The teachings of the Catholic Church receive enormous support from findings in psychiatry, psychology and related fields. For example, on aspects of marriage:

"There is almost universal agreement among therapists that conflict is inevitable in a marriage… when, following the honeymoon, couples have to make unromantic decisions (when to visit in-laws, how to budget money, etc.). Authorities agree that it is how couples deal with such inherent conflicts that determine the quality and duration of their relationship."[17]

The research suggests that the psychological factors most directly implicated in the development of a satisfactory marital relationship include:

1. A perception of being loved.

2. Agreement over central issues.

3. Procedures for resolving disagreements.

4. Emotional stability.

Studies conclude that marital satisfaction correlates with lower neuroticism, good impulse control and limited pre-marital sexual experience. Unhappy couples are more likely to reciprocate negative behaviour, to disagree often and to use sarcasm as a means of communication. Among the 'myths' which lead to marital disharmony are:

1. The idea that spouses are not capable of adapting to new circumstances.

2. The idea that one's spouse should know one's feelings and thoughts and it is therefore unimportant to communicate them.

3. The idea that a perfect sex life can guarantee marital stability.[18]

Aspects of family life

Again we note that the research findings regarding family life are in harmony with the teaching of the Church: "In the field of delinquency, especially in girls, the view that a broken home plays an important role is strong and consistent."[19]

The role that separation and divorce play in fostering conduct disorder in young people (that is, aggression, lying, destructive behaviour, vandalism, theft and truancy) was demonstrated by psychiatrist Sir Michael Rutter in a famous study in 1971 and has been confirmed by subsequent studies:

"Families broken by divorce and separation produce antisocial children rather than those broken by parental death…stealing and unsocialised aggression relate to a failure to discover a secure relationship with an adult."[20]

A study carried out many years ago concluded that risk factors for suicide in children and young people include parental divorce, depression and feelings of being abandoned.[21]

So we have known for a considerable period of time that stable couples tend to bring up stable children. However, we will now show that some of the more severe mental disorders have a biological cause, and so some people may develop a mental illness even if they come from a stable background.

An Introduction to Some Psychiatric Disorders

The purpose of this section is to show that mental illness is as serious as heart disease or cancer. In fact, considering heart disease might help us better understand mental illness: a person may develop heart disease for a variety of reasons including obesity, smoking and a genetic predisposition.

Similarly, it is helpful to think of mental illness as being brought about by different reasons including genetic and environmental ones. If the cause is identified correctly, the correct treatment can be offered. In practice, however, it is likely that there will be more than one cause for a particular episode of mental illness.

Understanding depression

Depression is a common psychiatric disorder affecting 10 per cent of the UK population at any one time. Women are more affected than men. It appears to be becoming more common, but this may be because of better detection and greater willingness to seek help. Most patients with depression are treated by their GP.

Depression is experienced as a prolonged state of misery, loss of hope in the future, sleep disturbance, change of weight and inability to cope with daily living. It is therefore more than a passing sadness.

In his excellent book *The Catholic Guide to Depression*, Dr Aaron Kheriaty writes:

> "The causes of depression are complex, and many individuals come into the world with strong genetic or environmental causes, which manifest regardless of the individual's life circumstances or choices and regardless of how much the individuals pray or how virtuous they are. Many religiously devout and even saintly individuals suffered from severe depression."[22]

Today, psychiatrists ought to understand depression from a biological, psychological, social and spiritual perspective. The spiritual perspective, generally ignored, is important, as Dr Kheriaty quotes a 1995 study which shows that 80 per cent of patients with a mental illness considered themselves spiritual or religious and 48 per cent of them considered themselves deeply religious. Thirty-eight per cent found it uncomfortable to mention their religious beliefs to their therapist. This may not be surprising, as Dr Kheriaty also notes that psychiatrists, psychologists and other mental health professionals tend to be less religious than the general population.

Dr Kheriaty documents that 72 per cent of studies show that religious beliefs have a beneficial effect on mental health. This suggests the importance of people with depression talking about their spiritual needs, as they often feel not only cut off from themselves but from others and from God as well. Even though they need the company of others and God, the nature of depression is such as to render them unable to express this need, the very need that might bring them hope and healing.

With advances in brain science, psychiatrists have moved from a psychotherapeutic approach to a more biological and medical approach in the treatment of depression. It is recognised that there is a change in the brain chemistry when a person suffers depression. Anti-depressants may therefore be a good option when prescribed appropriately. It is also recognised that the way we think can also change the brain chemistry. Therefore treatments such as cognitive therapy, which changes the way we think, can also help in the treatment of depression.

In many instances, this medical and brief psychological model appears to work. But these days there appears to be little space for "those less quantifiable aspects of care such as the quest for hope, the search for meaning, and the possibility of a loving relationship with a transcendent God."[23]

It is also possible that when the medical model is over-emphasised, people troubled because they are seeking a spiritual meaning to their lives may be misdiagnosed as having depression and treated inappropriately with anti-depressants. Or perhaps they do have depression but not the type that responds to anti-depressants.

So a holistic approach to the treatment of depression should mean that spirituality needs to be taken into consideration. To quote Dr Kheriaty:

"Depression need not utterly overwhelm those who are united to God. Instead of indicating separation from God, suffering can become a vehicle by which one is brought into deep intimacy with Him. Human suffering can have sanctifying value when united to the sufferings of Christ. For the first time since the Fall the human race does not have to be irredeemably sad. We need not give into despair."

What a pity it is that this vision of the human person and of suffering is hardly heard of these days outside of our churches. How useful it would be to construct a synthesis of mental-health treatments and authentic Catholic spirituality.

Some Catholics assume that depression is the result of a moral fault or spiritual failure. It is true that all sicknesses and sin are due to the original sin of our first parents. However, from this it does not follow that depression is always due to personal sin.

Some Catholics appear to confuse depression with the dark night of the soul as described by St John of the Cross. They are not the same. The dark night is a grace given by

God to purify the soul, to make the person more selfless and more abandoned to God. The problem with confusing the dark night of the soul with depression is that there is a real danger that the person suffering from depression may not receive the right treatment at the right time.

Helping people through depression almost always means more than prescribing anti-depressants. Understanding depression has made us realise the importance of friendship with others and with God. Many of us can suffer depression when we have to come to terms with loss. It is perhaps during these times that we mature spiritually.

However, some people with severe depression may develop suicidal thoughts or psychosis and they need urgent medical attention. About 10 per cent of those who are depressed die by suicide. The psychotic symptoms of depression include delusions (fixed false beliefs out of keeping with the person's cultural background) that they are worthless or that they are dying. They may have hallucinations (typically voices talking to them when there is nobody there) that are unpleasant. They may think, for example, that they are hearing voices telling them: "you are evil", or "you should not be alive".

It is possible for such severely depressed persons to find comfort and hope in the Catholic spiritual tradition, but this should be seen as an adjunct to medical attention. If the sufferer starts dwelling on his delusions (that he is useless or beyond redemption), it is better not to reason with him but to move the conversation to the goodness and mercy of God: the deluded person, by definition, is beyond reason.

If a person confesses the sin of despair frequently and gains no comfort whatever from the priest's words on the mercy of God, he is likely to be suffering from a depressive illness that requires medical help. A depressed person is inhibited in his emotional life and, in consequence, his emotions will not reach out to God. If he is to fall in love with the God who has seemingly burdened him with such a heavy cross, he has a special need to see the loving kindness of God reflected in the face of another human being.

Anne

Anne is a Catholic who had attended Mass two or three times a week. She and her husband had problems conceiving, but at the age of 35 she gave birth to her only child. Several years later, he was knocked down by a car and killed.

Three months later, her GP decided that she was depressed enough to warrant a course of anti-depressants. There was only a slight improvement and she was therefore referred to a psychiatrist. At that time she was not only depressed but was also very angry - angry with herself, with the driver and with God. She stopped going to church because she felt she was being a hypocrite.

In our secular age, it is difficult for a psychiatrist to ask a vulnerable patient about her religious beliefs. Anne did not start talking about her beliefs until the psychiatrist asked the following open and non-threatening question: "Do you have any religious or spiritual beliefs?"

As soon as the question was asked, it was quite clear that Anne did want to talk about her religious beliefs and about her apparent loss of faith. After a few reviews, she said that she had found it helpful to talk to someone who shared her beliefs and she also said that she was ready to see a priest.

Sometime later, she had returned to church. She was not back to her previous self and perhaps she will never fully recover, but she had regained the will to live again.

In Anne's case, a purely medical approach to treatment proved unhelpful, but there was improvement when medical care was combined with spiritual care.

Amy

Amy is eighty years old. She had been attending Mass every day. Her husband had died recently and she had since then been feeling low in mood. Her daughter thought that this was normal grief, but then Amy started hearing voices telling her that she was evil. She felt hopeless and claimed that she had lost her faith.

Amy was not only depressed but, unlike Anne, she also had psychotic symptoms. She was too ill to find spiritual guidance helpful, but she did respond to medical treatment and, while briefly hospitalised, she received Holy Communion regularly.

After making a recovery, she thanked those who looked after her - especially those who helped her spiritually.

Brenda

After Brenda had an abortion, she started feeling low in mood. The GP diagnosed her as having depression for no obvious reason and started her on anti-depressants. This made no difference.

She felt withdrawn and numb. She also had recurrent nightmares. A friend suggested that she see a pro-life counsellor.

A few months later, Brenda still had occasional nightmares about the abortion but was much improved. She felt a need to ask the aborted child for forgiveness.

It would appear that Brenda's doctor had not recognised that her depression was caused by the abortion. Without identifying the cause, it is difficult to offer the right help.

Catherine

Catherine attended Mass daily. There is a strong family history of mental illness. Her brother was diagnosed with bipolar disorder and committed suicide when in his twenties.

Catherine has been feeling depressed and hopeless for some months. A friend suggests that the problem might be spiritual and that she is entering the dark night of the soul. However, now Catherine develops persistent thoughts of wanting to harm herself and she even plans out how she might do this.

Catherine had the good sense to see her GP who put her on medication and referred her to a specialist.

Catherine had wanted to see a specialist who shared her beliefs, but in her case it was far more important to see a competent clinician than one who shared her beliefs. Besides, there are not that many fully believing Catholic psychiatrists around.

David

David is eighty years old. His wife died recently and he is finding it difficult to care for himself. His children live a long way from him and there is little contact. He also has little contact with his busy neighbours. He can no longer go to Mass as he can no longer drive.

Because he appears to be low in mood, he is prescribed anti-depressants.

The case of David occurred twenty years ago. Clearly what David needed was social care, and one can but hope that such inappropriate medical interventions are rare these days. Such cases were far from uncommon and they go a long way to help explain why some people dismiss the whole of psychiatry as fraudulent.

Fred

Fred is fifty years old. His wife has finally left him after tolerating years of infidelity. The GP refers him to a psychiatrist because Fred has been feeling low in mood and has not responded to anti-depressants.

When assessed, there was no evidence of depression. Fred said that he was looking for "someone wise" to help him find meaning to his life.

When should a psychiatrist recommend spiritual guidance to a patient? In Fred's case the anti-depressant was withdrawn without difficulty and he gained enough insight to realise that he was in fact looking for spiritual help.

George

George has retired from his business. He has been treated for depression for some months without success. It is initially thought that he has delusions about swindling people. Later it transpires that his business ethics had been far from sound. He now feels guilty and he wishes to make up for his past.

George had enough insight to realise that he needed recourse to the sacraments. Pope Pius XII said: "No one can deny that there can exist an irrational and even morbid sense of guilt. But a person may also be aware of a real fault which has not been wiped away."

Arlen Bonnar, a moral theologian, wrote: "Confession, even though it belongs to the supernatural order, helps to dissipate neurosis by taking away the guilt of sin, so potent a factor in the development of many neuroses."[24]

In this section, we have seen that depression is sometimes incorrectly diagnosed. Depression has a variety of different causes and it is therefore possible to offer the wrong treatment if the right cause has not been identified.

Understanding obsessive-compulsive disorder and scruples

Obsessive-compulsive disorder (OCD) is a form of anxiety disorder in which a person suffers from thoughts which repeatedly and persistently come into his mind and interfere with normal thought, leading to anxiety, which can also lead to repetitive behaviour aimed at reducing the anxiety.

The thoughts may be violent, blasphemous or obscene in content. The sufferer realises that they are his own thoughts and he also recognises the absurdity of these thoughts - this makes this illness particularly distressing. For example, he may fear contamination and carry out the compulsive ritual of hand washing. This may lead to a brief period of reduced anxiety until the thoughts and rituals are repeated. The frequent performance of rituals does not relieve anxiety but increases it.

About 1 per cent of the population have OCD at any one time. It may begin in adolescence or early adulthood, although it may be some years before the sufferer seeks help.

Anti-depressant tablets can sometimes help, as can various psychological therapies. The sufferer constantly has to make choices between two responses, both of which lead to anxiety. He must have complete confidence in the therapist and believe that he has been taken seriously in face of the absurdity he may feel.

Some people who have scruples have sufficient symptoms to warrant a diagnosis of OCD. Scruples may be defined as an unreasonable fear of sin, producing spiritual anguish. The anguish causes the person to see sin where there is no sin. Far from being a sign of sanctity, scruples are to be regarded as a spiritual affliction, although it is true that a number of saints suffered from them at some stage in their spiritual lives: St Ignatius of Loyola and St Francis de Sales, for example. Once the sufferer recognises his spiritual blindness, he is not only on the road to recovery but is possibly moving towards the heights of sanctity. Unfortunately, if obedience is lacking, scruples can weary the mind, make piety a burden and pave the way to tepidity.

Great damage can be done to the interior life because of obsessive fears and doubts.

Writing over a hundred years ago, the Jesuit Fr De Lehen recommended sufferers of obsessional thoughts not to "protest energetically…[A] contemptuous turning away is the most efficacious." He also recommended the following:

1. Submit all to the judgement of the spiritual director. Without this obedience (and in the absence of mental illness which may require a different remedy) the sufferers are unlikely to be cured. They must learn to sacrifice their own doubts. Otherwise, "they wander with their difficulties of conscience from confessional to confessional…nothing so impairs peace as these unending consultations."

2. The sufferer must keep himself occupied, especially with manual labour and works of mercy.

3. He should keep cheerful company with friends and learn not to take himself too seriously.

4. He should develop a childlike simplicity and learn not to be surprised if he has a relapse. The humble man is not shocked by his own weakness.[25]

Theologians have long known that scruples may be due to mental illness. The Dominican theologian St Antoninus of Florence (1389-1459) wrote: "Scruples often arise from depression in which the imagination and, sometimes, even reason are disturbed."

Harry

Harry is a fifty-year-old man with OCD and the condition had crippled his life. For example, he had to carry out a whole series of rituals before leaving home. In his case, response to anti-depressants had been poor and psychological remedies were only marginally better. He was quite a challenge to priests as he was never reassured after he had confessed.

Then Harry met a priest whom he was able to trust completely. He also felt the same way towards a therapist. He began to realise that previously he had wanted to control everything in his life. He had wanted to be a 'super perfectionist' and act almost like God. This was obviously not possible and so he started making simple acts of abandonment to God. He no longer checked the lights fifty times because he said to himself that the worst that might happen was that he might end up with a hefty electricity bill. What really mattered was his relationship with God. He spoke about these things both with his priest and with his therapist.

Here we see a beautiful harmony between Catholic spirituality and psychiatry. This synthesis may not help all people with the more severe form of OCD, but it most certainly helped Harry.

Understanding schizophrenia

In 1911, the psychiatrist Eugen Bleuler coined the term 'schizophrenia' which literally means 'shattered mind'. Schizophrenia is a psychiatric illness characterised by delusions, hallucinations and a disturbed mental process. In some cases, it is a chronic condition and can leave residual psychiatric symptoms and impaired social functioning. Illness rates are higher in lower social classes, but this may reflect the tendency of the sufferer to drift down the social scale.

Most studies show a lifetime prevalence of about 1 per cent for schizophrenia. Although there appear to be many causes of the illness, genetic factors have been identified and it is now regarded as being due to abnormal brain activity. The theory that parents cause the illness by the way they interact with children, a theory that led to enormous guilt, is no longer accepted.

There are different types of this condition. Paranoid schizophrenia is the most common form and is characterised by delusions of persecution and unpleasant hallucinatory voices. Residual schizophrenia is characterised by social isolation, withdrawal and emotional blunting.

The person suffering from schizophrenia may feel that his thoughts are being put into his mind by external forces or that they are being removed. He may feel that his thoughts are freely communicated to other people. A failure of logical connection between one thought and another may lead to odd changes in conversation.

The person with schizophrenia is likely to benefit from anti-psychotic medication and psychological interventions. He may require some practical guidance in daily living and some form of sheltered work as part of his rehabilitation.

Although there have been recent well-documented cases of dangerous behaviour in this group, the typical sufferer is much more likely to be a vulnerable, isolated person who finds the world as bizarre as the world may find him. About 10 per cent of people with schizophrenia end their lives by means of suicide.

Those who are called to care for people with schizophrenia ought to do so with prudence. Without dismissing the sufferer's delusions and without reinforcing them, they can remind him of the love of God and of the importance of daily activities as well as helping him towards a more realistic understanding of the nature of his experience. Roger Grainger, a hospital chaplain, wrote:

> "A particular kind of listening is called for in such cases, one which makes as clear as possible the precise nature of the support you are offering. You have to get across the fact that you aren't questioning the presence of the delusion, nor the misery it causes, only its independent existence. Whatever it is is part of them. Your concern is for the whole person, voices and all."[26]

Ian

Ian is a twenty-year-old student. He has become more withdrawn in the last few months, he mutters to himself and he appears preoccupied and agitated. Although not at all religious, he goes to see the local Catholic priest and asks for exorcism as he feels that the devil is interfering with his thoughts. He can also hear the devil telling him to end his life.

The priest immediately advised Ian to seek medical help and Ian had to be hospitalised. He responded well to drug treatment and psychological therapy.

Roger

Roger is one of the holiest men the author has had the privilege of meeting. He has a diagnosis of chronic schizophrenia and the illness has never really responded fully to treatment. Roger goes to Mass daily almost without fail. He sometimes talks to himself during Mass. However, when it comes to Holy Communion, he exhibits an incredible degree of recollection. His faith is uncomplicated. He has an extraordinary degree of humility and he has no self-pity or bitterness about his illness.

Roger is a great example of how faith should be lived and he has brought many others close to God.

The person suffering from schizophrenia can most certainly benefit from both medical and spiritual care.

Understanding addictions

A quarter of adults in England consume alcohol at hazardous levels, the number of dependent drinkers stands at 1.6 million and the number that go into hospital for alcohol-related reasons rose by 52 per cent between 1996 and 2006. Men are more affected than women, but the frequency of female cases of alcoholism is increasing.

There is evidence that heavy drinking runs in families. Twin studies and adoption studies support the hypothesis of a genetic predisposition to developing alcoholism. However, a predisposition does not mean that the person is compelled to become an addict.

It has been argued that alcoholism is not in itself a disease but a behaviour that can be controlled with appropriate help. The psychiatrist Professor Tom Burns writes:

"The rebranding of addiction as illness was a humanitarian impulse in the 1940s after the founding of Alcoholics Anonymous in 1939, to provide help to detoxify addicted individuals and support society. The world's largest self-help groups (Alcoholics Anonymous, Narcotics Anonymous) both consider addiction a lifelong illness, although they rely on personal and spiritual support rather than medical treatment."[27]

So it could be argued that it is far from clear what a psychiatrist's role should be in the treatment of addictions. Most addicts do not have a mental illness and many overcome their addiction without psychiatric help. However, it could be argued that there are good reasons for psychiatric involvement: people with mental health problems have an increased risk of becoming addicts and addiction may cause depression and other mental-health problems.

There are social, psychological and spiritual causes of addiction. According to an article published in the *British Journal of Psychiatry*, religious people are less likely to have problems with drug and alcohol dependence.[28]

People may drink excessively in order to alleviate stress. Some people drink because they suffer from social phobia, becoming anxious when they are put in situations with other people. The social consequences of alcoholism include marital breakdown, violence, crime and unemployment. Suicide is the cause of death in about 15 per cent of alcoholics.

A person who is dependent on alcohol is likely to suffer from withdrawal symptoms such as tremor and anxiety and he is more likely to drink in order to relieve these symptoms. Drink becomes the primary event in his life and he is unable to vary the amount of alcohol according to social circumstances.

Once he has been detoxified, possibly with medical treatment, the person will need to take a good look at his life. He may have to avoid certain places and people associated with his past life, and he may find support groups such as Alcoholics Anonymous helpful.

It is generally not recommended for a reformed alcoholic to resume social drinking. The first drink may affect his judgement and weaken his willpower. It is, however, not uncommon for him to suffer a relapse. The sacraments and a complete confidence in God may help him in his battle against addiction.

Grace is stronger than his weakness. The relapsed alcoholic often feels hopeless and he needs the appropriate psychological and spiritual help in order to increase his sense of self-worth.

John

John has been drinking off and on for twenty years. He goes to see his psychiatrist and tells him: "It has been three months since I last saw you. In that time I have had two relapses and I am really sorry that this has happened."

This sounds rather like a confession. It is a reminder that addictions may be regarded as moral disorders with physical and psychological consequences.

The saintly Matt Talbot responded to his alcoholism by living well the Act of Contrition: being sorry for his sins, detesting them above all things, resolving never to offend again and carefully avoiding occasions of sin. To a significant extent, this is a summary of the management of alcohol dependence. Strong motivation leads to a good outcome. Matt Talbot was very strongly motivated: he fell in love with God.

It could be argued that John would benefit more by seeing a priest than a psychiatrist. However, John needed both priest and psychiatrist especially at the beginning of rehabilitation. He then joined Alcoholics Anonymous and he believes that this organisation has saved his life. It is fair to say that others do not find Alcoholics Anonymous as helpful.

Ken

Ken is a family man for whom his wife and children come first. He is introduced to the drug heroin and soon becomes an addict. He tries to keep this a secret from his wife but she finds out and is horrified. She tells him that she will leave him unless he gives up the drug.

Ken really wanted to overcome his addiction. He first tried doing so on his own but failed. He then went to see a specialist who put him on reducing doses of an alternative drug. During this time he went regularly to confession and he received spiritual direction. He was soon free from drug addiction.

Again we see the importance of motivation, family support and spiritual help. His wife may have reacted angrily to begin with, but she was very supportive throughout his time of rehabilitation. We see here again the wonderful harmony between psychiatric and spiritual care.

Understanding suicide

The number of people taking their own lives in the UK rose significantly in 2011. Some 6045 people killed themselves that year, an increase of 437 since 2010. The highest suicide rate was among men aged 30 to 44.

Certain groups are at greater risk of dying by suicide:

1. People with mental illness, especially depression and alcoholism.
2. People with a family history of suicide.
3. People with chronic physical ill health.
4. People who are unemployed.
5. People who are older.
6. People from a broken home.
7. People with a history of suicide attempts.

There also appears to be a greater risk after the death of one's spouse. Studies have consistently shown a correlation between suicide and social isolation.

Two-thirds of all those who die by suicide consult their GPs in the week before taking their own lives. About 90 per cent would have had a mental illness at some time, although the illness may not have been recognised and adequately treated.

Protective factors against suicide include being religious and having a supportive family.

Good psychiatric practice does not contravene sound ethical principles. Suicide is a violation of a human good and can never be regarded as an appropriate course of action. All that psychiatry can demonstrate is the diminution of moral responsibility based on a person's mental state when committing the act.

Lorna

Lorna was just twenty-seven years old when she took her own life. She was diagnosed with depression four years previously and it had not really responded to treatment. She had become even more depressed after splitting up with her boyfriend. She took an overdose of tablets and by the time she was found, she had been dead for some time. Her parents were devastated. They described themselves, at the time, as having died with their daughter.

The Church teaches that grave psychological disturbances can diminish the responsibility of the one dying by suicide. Therefore we should not despair of the eternal salvation of persons who have taken their own lives. In the case of Lorna, there is little doubt that responsibility for her action had been diminished by severe depression.

How ought we to deal with Lorna's grieving parents? Dr Kheriaty writes:

> "If a person is not clinically depressed, a medical or therapeutic approach to bereavement may not prove the most helpful. Surrounding yourself with loving and supportive family members and pouring out your heart in prayer consistently and patiently is the only real advice I can offer."

The majority of people who are at risk of killing themselves have a treatable mental-health problem. It is imperative for them to access appropriate services.

Conclusion

Macbeth: Canst thou not minister to a mind diseased,
       Pluck from the memory a rooted sorrow,
       Raze out the written trouble of the brain,
       And with some sweet, oblivious antidote
       Cleanse the stuff'd bosom of that perilous stuff
       Which weighs upon the heart?

Doctor: Therein the patient Must minister to himself.

We need not be as negative as the doctor in Shakespeare's *Macbeth*. Truth can never be in conflict with itself. There is harmony between faith and reason, theology and science, Catholicism and psychiatry. Our understanding of mental illness can be more complete if we draw upon the insight of both medicine and Catholicism.

A psychiatrist is a 'doctor of the soul', but in modern psychiatry the original meaning has been abandoned and psychiatrists tend to focus on the body, and especially the brain, to the exclusion of the soul. There is a real need now for Catholic spirituality to accompany the medical approach to the care of the mentally ill.

Endnotes

[1] Auton, N., *The Pastoral Care of the Mentally Ill* (London, SPCK, 1963)

[2] Quoted in Dominian, J., *Depression* (London, Fontana Press, 1976)

[3] Braceland, F. and Stock, M., *Modern Psychiatry* (Garden City, NY, Image Books, 1966)

[4] Quoted in Fish, F., *Outline of Psychiatry* (Oxford, Butterworth-Heinemann, 1984)

[5] Quoted in O'Doherty, E.F. and McGrath, S.D., *The Priest and Mental Health* (New York, NY, Alba, 1963)

[6] Sims, A., *Symptoms in the Mind* (London, Ballière Tindall, 1987)

[7] Vitz, P., *Sigmund Freud's Christian Unconscious* (Leominster, UK, Gracewing, 1993)

[8] Thornton, E.M., *The Freudian Fallacy* (London, Grafton, 1986)

[9] Storr, A., *Jung* (London, Fontana Press, 2008)

[10] Deutsch, H., *The Psychology of Women* (New York, NY, Allyn and Bacon, 1945)

[11] Duffey, F.D., *Psychiatry and Asceticism* (Roman Catholic Books, 2006)

[12] Quoted in O'Doherty, E.F., *Religion and Personality Problems* (Staten Island, NY, Alba, 1965)

[13] Kretschmer, E., *The Psychology of Men of Genius* (Washington, McGrath, 1970)

[14] Fish, F., *Fish's Clinical Psychopathology* (Bristol, John Wright and Sons, 1985)

[15] Quoted in *Religion and Personality Problems*, (n 12)

[16] VanderVeldt, J.H. and Odenwald, R., *Psychiatry and Catholicism* (New York, NY, McGraw-Hill, 1952)

[17] Davison, G. and Neale, J., *Abnormal Psychology* (New York, NY, John Wiley, 2001)

[18] Adapted from Tantam, D. and Birchwood, M., *Seminars in Psychology and Social Sciences* (London, Gaskell, 1994)

[19] Slater, E. and Roth, M., *Clinical Psychiatry* (London, Cassell, 1961)

[20] Hill, P., Murray, R. and Thorley, A., *Essentials of Postgraduate Psychiatry* (London, Grune and Stratton, 1986)

[21] Shaffer, D., 'Suicide in children and young adolescents', *Journal of the American Academy of Child Psychiatry*, 15, 1974, pp. 275-91

[22] Kheriaty, A. and Cihak, J., *The Catholic Guide to Depression* (USA, Sophia Institute Press, 2012)

[23] Swinton, J., *Spirituality and Mental Health Care: Rediscovering the Forgotten Dimension* (London, Jessica Kingsley Publishers, 2004)

[24] Bonnar, A., *The Catholic Doctor* (London, Burns, Oates and Washbourne, 1944)

[25] de Lehen, E., *The Way of Interior Peace* (New York, Benziger Brothers, 1888)

[26] Grainger, R., *Strangers in the Pews* (London, Epworth Press, 1993)

[27] Burns, T., *Psychiatry: A Very Short Introduction* (Oxford, OUP, 2006)

[28] King, M., 'Religion, Spirituality and Mental Health', *British Journal of Psychiatry* 202, 2013, pp. 68-73

Giving Meaning to Suffering

Guido Davanzo

In one way or another suffering and death are inevitable realities that we encounter in the course of our existence. Christ gave a meaning to all human suffering by going through it himself, and transforming its consequences.

This booklet looks at the psychological and spiritual effects of sickness and suffering and gives the good news that Jesus can make even our suffering glorious.

PA4   ISBN 978 1 86082 326 8

The Catholic Church
& the Sex Abuse Crisis

Dr Pravin Thevathasan

This excellently researched booklet sets out the nature
and extent of clerical sexual abuse, its prevalence, likely
causes and consequences. Its robust analysis of the
crisis and its handling by Church authorities is both
illuminating and balanced. The position, teaching and
pastoral response to the crisis of the Catholic Church are
rigorously assessed.

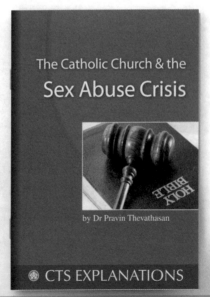

Ex39   ISBN 978 1 86082 749 5

Catholic Social Teaching

Stratford Caldecott

'The Common Good', 'option for the poor' 'subsidiarity'-concepts like these have become part of the currency of Catholic teaching, but what do they mean? What are their foundations in scripture and tradition which make them distinctively Catholic?

This book examines key aspects of human social relations such as the family, the state and civil society, the world of work and justice. It explains in clear language how a conscience informed by divine revelation brings out the true human vocation to love of God and neighbour.

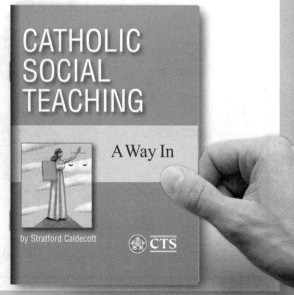

Do675   ISBN 978 1 86082 116 5